History Challenge

180 Brainteasers About the United States and the World

Arnold Cheyney

Good Year Books *An imprint of Addison-Wesley Educational Publishers, Inc.*

Good Year Books

are available for most basic curriculum subjects plus many enrichment areas. For more Good Year Books, contact your local bookseller or educational dealer. For a complete catalog with information about other Good Year Books, please write:

Good Year Books
1900 East Lake Avenue
Glenview, IL 60025

Book design and illustration by Nancy Rudd.
Copyright © 1999 Good Year Books, an imprint of Addison-Wesley Educational Publishers, Inc.
All Rights Reserved.
Printed in the United States of America.

ISBN 0-673-36382-1

1 2 3 4 5 6 7 8 9 SO 06 05 04 03 02 01 00 99

Scientists believe there was a land bridge many years ago connecting Russia to Alaska. People probably traveled across it and entered North America. What separates Russia and Alaska now?

After being imprisoned for many years in South Africa, Nelson Mandela was set free. What position of leadership did he attain in South Africa?

Pyramids built by Indians in South and Central America were shaped differently than those built in Egypt. How were America's pyramids different in shape from those in Egypt?

The Persian Gulf War began when Iraq invaded Kuwait in 1990. Egypt, France, Great Britain, Saudi Arabia, Syria, and the United States sided with Kuwait. What was another name for this war?

The Great Sphinx in Egypt was constructed about 4,500 years ago. The Sphinx supposedly asked passers-by this riddle: What has one voice, becomes four-footed, is then two-footed, and then becomes three-footed? What is the answer?

On April 12, 1981, a space shuttle was launched by the United States. A space shuttle is a reusable manned spacecraft that can return to Earth and be sent back into space again with astronauts. What was the name of the first space shuttle?

A large ring of huge stones was erected in southwestern England between 2800 and 1500 B.C. People probably used the ring for their religious ceremonies. What is the place now called?

The nine members of the United States Supreme Court had always been men until 1981. Who was President at that time, and what did he do to change the Supreme Court?

Herodotus, the first Greek historian, described Persian messengers in these words: "Neither snow / nor rain / nor heat / nor gloom of night stays these couriers from the swift completion of their appointed rounds." On what federal building in New York City are these words inscribed?

Although a few women had completed their husbands' terms of office in the Senate after their spouses passed away, this woman was the first elected full-term female Senator. Who is she, and what state is she from?

The Great Wall of China, designed to stop Mongol invaders from the north, is 4,000 miles (6,400 kilometers) long. Now that the wall is not used for defense, what purpose does it serve?

President Richard M. Nixon resigned from office August 9, 1974, because of a scandal surrounding a break-in at the Democratic national headquarters. What was the scandal called?

Writing is one of the greatest achievements in the history of the world. The Sumerians, around 3500 B.C., invented the first writing by making wedge-shaped symbols in wet clay. What were these symbols called?

The hydrogen bomb is much more powerful than the atomic bomb. What is the process called that combines hydrogen atoms to make an explosion?

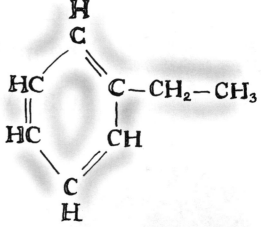

History Challenge

After a famine hit Canaan, the Israelites migrated to Egypt and lived there peacefully for many centuries until the thirteenth century B.C. Who led them back to Canaan?

LEVEL 2

8

The first person to set foot on the moon was astronaut Neil Armstrong on July 20, 1969. At that time he said, "That's one small step for a man, one giant leap for mankind." What did he mean by that statement?

In 490 B.C. an Athenian runner, Pheidippides, ran from Marathon to Athens without stopping so he could proclaim an Athenian victory over Persia. How far did he run, and what happened to him?

In 1967 Dr. Christiaan Barnard performed the first human heart transplant by replacing the defective heart of a 55-year-old man with that of a healthy heart from a 25-year-old woman. Where did the surgery take place?

History Challenge

The Hanging Gardens of Babylon, which were created by King Nebuchadnezzar II in the sixth century B.C., are known as one of the Seven Wonders of the Ancient World. Nebuchadnezzar would at times go mad, thinking he was an ox. What would he eat at those times?

The longest war in which the United States was involved took place in Southeast Asia. What was the war?

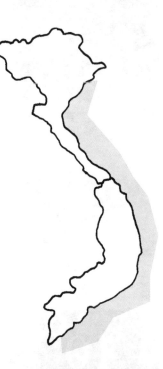

Buddha, founder of Buddhism, lived in India around 500 B.C. He believed that by meditating, people could be released from suffering and find harmony and joy in their lives. What is this state called?

Biologist and science writer Rachel Carson wrote a book, *Silent Spring,* which told how some pesticides kill not only insects but birds in the same area. What are the initials of a dangerous pesticide Rachel warned about in her book?

Alexander the Great, in the fourth century B.C., was 20 years old when he became king of the Macedonians and 32 years old when he died. He conquered Asia Minor, Syria, Egypt, Babylonia, and Persia. Who was the Greek philosopher who was his tutor?

"I have a dream . . . that my four little children will one day live in a nation where they will not be judged by the color of their skin but by the content of their character." Who made this statement?

The famous Alexandrian Library, founded by Alexander the Great in 330 B.C., contained over 400,000 scrolls. On what were they written?

The Berlin Wall, erected by the East German Communist government in August 1961, separated the city of East Berlin from noncommunist West Berlin. Over 170 people died trying to escape from East Berlin, many shot by border guards. When was the wall dismantled?

Julius Caesar, a Roman general, came to Egypt in 48 B.C. and defeated the guardians of the young king, Ptolemy. Whom did Caesar choose as the new ruler of Egypt?

The United States flag gained two stars in 1959. What states came into the United States of America at that time?

Confucius was a Chinese philosopher whose teachings influenced Chinese society from 100 B.C. to the early 1900s. His followers put his thoughts into a book. What is its title?

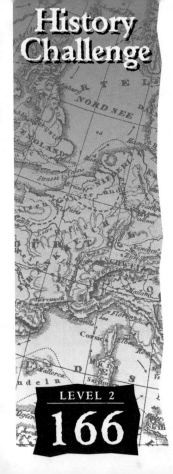

The Soviet Union launched the first man-made satellite into space in 1957. What was it called?

Hippocrates, the father of the scientific study of medicine, headed a school for physicians in Greece, where he wrote many volumes on medicine. What were these called?

"Ask not what your country can do for you. Ask what you can do for your country." What U.S. President made this statement in his inaugural address?

Galen, a famous early physician, discovered by treating the wounds of men who battled each other in coliseums that blood runs through arteries. What was the profession of these men?

The Congress of Industrial Organizations (CIO) was a union that organized all the workers in a plant into one union. In 1955 the CIO merged with another union. What did the combined organizations become?

Constantine was emperor of the Roman Empire in the early fourth century A.D. The capital of the empire was Constantinople. What is the city now called, and in what country is it found?

Charles De Gaulle, a French statesman and soldier, fought against Germany in World War II and later led France as its president. What is the ancient Roman name for France?

In A.D. 528 Emperor Justinian I, head of the Byzantine (East Roman) Empire, appointed a committee to update and summarize all Roman laws. What did this collection of laws become known as?

During World War II, George C. Marshall commanded the largest army the United States had ever amassed and later, in 1953, won the Nobel Peace Prize. What did he do to receive the Nobel Peace Prize?

Islam, one of the world's largest religions, was begun by the Prophet Muhammad in the seventh century A.D. What are those who worship Islam called?

Many well-known Americans and people in government in the early 1950s were falsely accused of being Communists by a U.S. senator. What was the accuser's name?

About the year A.D. 1002, a Norse explorer, Leif Eriksson, sailed to Newfoundland where he found lumber for building ships, and grapes. What did he name the new land?

Rock music began in the 1950s as "rock and roll" and soon became an international music form. Who was rock music's first superstar?

Beginning in A.D. 1173 and ending between 1360 and 1370, a bell tower was constructed on soft ground in Italy. It is seven-stories high and has 300 steps that lead to the top story. What is this building called?

Sir Winston Churchill, prime minister of England during World War II, used the term Iron Curtain in a speech at Westminster College in Fulton, Missouri, on March 5, 1946. The Iron Curtain separated what kinds of governments?

The Magna Carta (Great Charter) of 1215 guaranteed basic rights in England. What effect has the document had on the United States?

Oak Ridge National Laboratory in Oak Ridge, Tennessee, was built in World War II as part of the Manhattan Project. What was built there?

Indians living in the southwestern United States from about A.D. 1000 to 1300 built their homes in canyon walls under the overhangs of rocks. What were these people called?

"The holocaust" is a term frequently used for the German Nazi party's killing of six million Jews and other peoples during World War II. What is the word for the systematic destruction of a people because of their religion, race, or nationality?

The Crusades were military expeditions in the Middle Ages led by European Christians intent on recapturing Palestine from the Muslims. Who made up the armies in the Crusades in 1212?

Harry S. Truman had been Vice-President for only 83 days when Franklin D. Roosevelt died. What was the most important decision Truman had to make?

Feudalism was a system in the Middle Ages that protected people in western Europe when there was no strong central government. A lord gave land (a fief) to a man for his loyalty and protection. What was the man called?

Up until the early 1900s the word *propaganda* meant "truth." A change of meaning came when V. I. Lenin led the Communist revolution that took over Russia. What has the word come to mean now?

History Challenge

Marco Polo, an Italian traveler in the 1200s, journeyed to China and back over the course of twenty-four years. What was China called in Marco Polo's time?

LEVEL 2

27

History Challenge

Winston Churchill brought the people of Great Britain together against the German dictator, Adolph Hitler, during World War II. What position did Churchill hold in Great Britain's government?

LEVEL 2

154

History
Challenge

Kublai Khan founded the Mongol dynasty
in China during the 1200s and 1300s.
Who was his grandfather?

One of the turning points in World War II was the Battle of Stalingrad in 1942 and 1943. This was as far as the Nazis could go into the Soviet Union. What is Stalingrad now called?

The Renaissance, a rebirth or revival of art and literature, began in Italy in the 1300s. Toward the end of the next century, who was the political and cultural leader of the Italian city of Florence?

Japanese threats to Hawaii were ended during World War II when the U.S. Pacific Fleet defeated a much larger Japanese array of ships in 1942. Near what island was the battle fought?

836

Michelangelo Buonarroti was an Italian sculptor, painter, architect, and poet who painted the Sistine Chapel in the Vatican. He also sculpted a famous king of Israel. Who was the king?

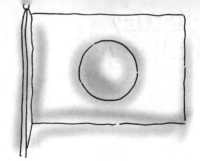

During World War II, the Japanese captured two islands in the Aleutian chain that are part of North America. These islands were the only land areas the Japanese were able to occupy in North America during that war. What are their names?

The plague known as the Black Death killed a quarter of the population of Europe in the middle 1300s. How was the disease transmitted to humans?

History Challenge

LEVEL 2

150

Eighteen-year-olds were first allowed to vote in 1943 in this Southern state. What is the state?

Joan of Arc, a French military leader and heroine, led French forces to victory over the English at the city of Orléans.

Later she was captured.

How did she die?

The first woman elected to both houses of the U.S. Congress was from Maine. What was her name?

The Treaty of Tordesillas in 1494 divided what is now Brazil between Spain and Portugal. What portion did Portugal receive?

Nellie T. Ross was the first woman governor of a state and later was appointed director of the United States Mint. Of what state was she governor, and what President appointed her as director of the United States Mint?

The King of France sent Jacques Cartier, a French navigator, to America to find gold in 1534. What he found was a large river that helped France in its claim of territory. What did he name the river?

Every day, investors buy and sell (trade) stock on exchanges such as the New York Stock Exchange in New York City. What are the market conditions called when stock prices rise? When they fall?

2589

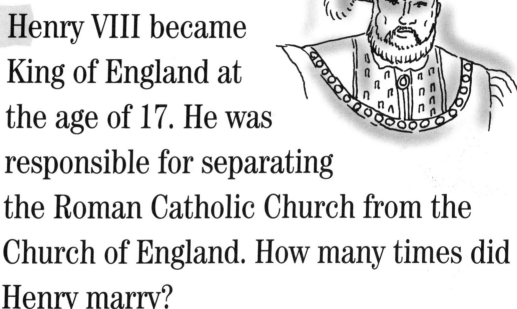

Henry VIII became King of England at the age of 17. He was responsible for separating the Roman Catholic Church from the Church of England. How many times did Henry marry?

Novels, such as *Main Street* and *Babbitt,* helped this writer in 1930 become the first American novelist to win the Nobel Prize for literature. Who was he?

Leonardo da Vinci was an Italian artist and inventor who put many of his observations and ideas into notebooks, which contain drawings on concepts such as machines that fly, parachutes, and a movable bridge. Of his work as an artist, what are his two most famous paintings?

The Great Depression of the 1930s was worldwide. What do most economists think started the Great Depression?

John Calvin, a leader in the Protestant Reformation, enlarged upon the idea that Christianity should reform society. What were Calvin's French followers called? his English followers?

Alexander Fleming (1881–1955), a British bacteriologist, found some green mold destroying bacteria in a culture plate in his laboratory. What life-saving antibiotic did this discovery lead to?

A German mapmaker, Martin Waldseemüller, suggested that an Italian-born explorer's name be used to designate the "New World" found by Christopher Columbus. What was the explorer's name?

Mary McLeod Bethune, an African American educator, was the founder of Bethune-Cookman College and worked in the administrations of four Presidents of the United States. Which Presidents did she serve?

A German monk protested certain practices of the Roman Catholic Church. This led to the Reformation, a religious movement begun in 1517, and Protestantism. What was the monk's name?

History Challenge

The first woman to become president of the Phillipines ran for president after her husband was assassinated during his bid for its presidency. What was her name?

142

A Portuguese explorer took the first European expedition around the southern tip of South America in 1520. What is the narrow waterway now called?

In 1926 Robert H. Goddard tested a rocket he designed and scared people for miles around when it fell to Earth and exploded. The publicity brought him funding to continue his experiments. What did Goddard's experiments finally result in doing?

The first European expedition to explore the Mississippi River was from Spain. The explorers came in 1541 searching for gold. Who was the leader?

Kemal Atatürk, founder and first president of modern Turkey, instituted a simple Roman alphabet and insisted that every Turk have a last name. The National Assembly gave him the last name *Atatürk*. What does "Atatürk" mean?

People of the Western world follow the Gregorian calendar of 1582, a calendar of 365 days in a year with a day added every fourth year. What is the year called when a day is added?

Sigmund Freud (1856–1939), Austrian physician and founder of psychoanalysis, believed that the mind can unconsciously repress memories going back to one's earliest days. The repressed memories can cause an illness. What did he call the illness?

History Challenge

LEVEL 2

43

In 1588 Spain was the world's most powerful nation. Spain's "Invincible Armada" was thought to be unstoppable. What country's fleet defeated the Spanish Armada?

In 1920 the United States granted women the right to vote. What amendment to the Constitution allowed women voting rights?

William Shakespeare was an English playwright, schoolteacher, and father of three children by his wife Anne Hathaway. What was the title of his famous tragedy about two young people?

The first person to fly alone across the Atlantic Ocean from the United States to Europe was Charles A. Lindbergh. What was the name of his plane?

The capital of the province of Quebec in Canada is the city of Quebec, the oldest city (1608) in Canada. The name *Quebec* comes from the Algonquian Indian language and means "the river narrows here." Who founded the city of Quebec?

Roald Amundsen of Norway and four other men were the first to reach the South Pole. Amundsen also crossed over the North Pole. What was his means of transportation over the North Pole?

History Challenge

LEVEL 2
46

The first white explorer and his crew to see what is now the state of Delaware arrived in 1609 from England. What was the explorer's name?

State prohibition laws against drinking alcoholic beverages preceded the passage of a similar amendment to the Constitution. This amendment was the only one ever repealed. What amendment was repealed?

In 1670 the Hudson's Bay Company began as a group of fur traders; now it is the world's largest fur-trading company. Two French fur traders and a group of Englishmen formed the company. Who were the Frenchmen?

Over the last few centuries, six different governments have ruled over what is now the state of Texas. What are the names of these governments?

The first permanent English settlers in America built a colony to look for gold. When none was found, to what cash crop did the colonists turn?

Radio became important to U.S. Presidents. What President was the first to have his inauguration described on radio, first to have one in the White House, and first to broadcast over radio?

The British established colonies along the eastern Atlantic coast of North America and in the Caribbean. How many colonies were in America?

World War I (1914–1918) began with the murder of Archduke Francis Ferdinand who was to be the next Austrian emperor. The killing took place in Sarajevo, Austria-Hungary. What Western Hemisphere country entered the war in 1917?

Many American colonists who were loyal to Great Britain during the Revolutionary War moved to Canada, where they received free land. What were these people called?

The largest person in physical size to be President of the United States was 6 feet tall and weighed more than 300 pounds.
Who was he?

The colonists in the thirteen colonies were taxed by the British without the colonists' consent. What did the colonists call this?

The first American motion-picture epic was a film made in 1915 about the American Civil War and its aftermath. What was it called?

René Descartes, a gifted mathematician and considered the father of modern philosophy, declared in Latin, "Cogito ergo sum," which translated means, "I think, therefore I am." What does this phrase mean to you?

On February 3, 1913, an amendment to the Constitution was ratified, allowing the federal government to collect taxes on income. What amendment was this?

Roger Williams believed the Indians should be paid for their land in Massachusetts, and people should have complete religious freedom. Massachusetts Bay Colony officials tried to send him back to England but he fled. What colony did he found?

This was the first U.S. President, while in office, to ride in an automobile, ride in an airplane, receive a Nobel prize, and submerge beneath the water in a submarine.

Who was he?

In his early twenties, Isaac Newton made three important discoveries: the theory of gravitation; the uncovering of the secrets of light and color; and the development of calculus, a kind of mathematics. What is the force that Newton discovered that keeps the Earth and moon in orbit around the sun?

Oliver Wendell Holmes, Jr., was the son of a famous writer and physician. After being seriously wounded three times during the Civil War, he studied law at Harvard. To what position did President Theodore Roosevelt appoint him?

The oldest institution of higher learning in the United States was founded in 1636 in Cambridge, Massachusetts.
What is its name?

Inexpensive automobiles and the gasoline to run them brought about the need for a harder rubber for tires. Charles Goodyear learned how to make rubber strong and resistant to heat and cold.
What is his method called?

Peter the Great, czar and then the first emperor of Russia, made his country into a powerful nation. Peter attempted to get Russians to "Westernize." What does this mean?

Historian and sociologist W. E. B. Du Bois, the first African American to receive a Ph.D. at Harvard, spoke out against racial discrimination. What organization did he found?

The first public school system in colonial America was established in 1647. Later, when the colony in which it was located became a state, it was the first to require children to go to school. What state is this?

Kitty Hawk, North Carolina, was the site of the first flight of a heavier-than-air machine. Who was the pilot of this successful effort in 1903?

In 1692 nineteen men and women were convicted of being witches and were hung in the Salem Massachusetts Bay Colony. One-hundred-fifty others were put in jail. What were these trials called?

Lord Baden-Powell, a British army general, began the Boy Scouts in 1907. With his sister, Agnes, he organized a similar group for girls. What was the girls' group first called?

HEAR YE!
HEAR YE!

Freedom to print what one believes to be the truth was upheld in the American colonies in 1735. A jury found printer John Peter Zenger not guilty for printing material opposing the British governor. What amendment to the Constitution gives the press freedom to print what it considers true?

In 1903 Marie Curie became the first woman to receive the Nobel Prize. In 1911 she won a second Nobel prize. For what did she receive the prizes?

Sixteen-year-old Eliza Lucas Pinckney took charge of her father's plantations in South Carolina in 1739 and developed a blue dye from plants. What was the dye called?

In 1896 this President was the first to use the telephone as a way of waging his political campaign. Who was he?

The Hartford Courant in Connecticut is the longest continuously published newspaper in the United States. In what year did the newspaper begin publication? When did your local newspaper begin publication?

TRIBUNE

Thomas A. Edison was a brilliant inventor, industrial leader, and researcher. He worked on electrical lighting, the telegraph, the telephone, the phonograph, and motion pictures. He did all this even though he had a physical handicap. What was his handicap?

In 1755 the British attempted to get the Acadians, people of French origin in northeastern Canada, to take an oath of allegiance to the British king. When they wouldn't, they were forced to move south, some of them going to New Orleans. What did those who went to New Orleans become known as?

The Apache warrior, Geronimo, fought settlers and soldiers in Mexico and the southwestern states for many years before he surrendered. Where and how did he spend his final years?

In 1776 at the age of nine, Andrew Jackson read the Declaration of Independence to his neighbors. As President of the United States, what was it that Jackson did about the national debt that no other President has been able to do?

History Challenge

Twenty-one-year-old May Folsom married a 49-year-old President of the United States and became the youngest First Lady in the country's history. Which President did she marry?

LEVEL 2
118

Many battles were fought in New Jersey during the Revolutionary War. Because the state and its people were so important in U.S. history, New Jersey was given a nickname. What is it?

During the 1800s, Susan B. Anthony supported causes such as the abolition of slavery, the abolishment of alcoholic beverages, and the right of women to vote. She was the first woman to be pictured on a U.S. coin in general circulation. What was the coin?

The French Revolution began on July 14, 1789. A prison fortress in Paris symbolized the oppressive government of King Louis XVI. Parisians captured the fortress and tore it down, and July 14 became French Independence Day.
What was the prison fortress called?

In the 1870s Elijah McCoy, an African American engineer, invented the lubricator cup, which continuously supplied oil to various parts of many machines. What expression may have come about when people insisted on having Elijah McCoy's invention on their equipment?

The French Revolution was over in 1799 and ended the rule of French kings. What French general took over the government at the end of the revolution?

Photographs of animals and people in motion were made by Eadweard Muybridge in the late 1800s by linking a number of cameras together and setting them off at rapid intervals as a subject passed by. What did Muybridge's project lead to?

Benjamin Banneker, an African American astronomer, farmer, mathematician, and surveyor, helped lay the boundaries for an important city in the United States. What was the city?

In 1898 the U.S. battleship *Maine* went to Havana, Cuba, to protect American citizens. The ship was mysteriously destroyed in an explosion, resulting in war with Spain. After defeating Spain, what land possessions did the United States receive?

In 1799, on a half-buried stone unearthed near Alexandria, Egypt, a message was found in three different languages. This stone became the key to the long-forgotten language of the ancient Egyptians. What was the name of the stone and in what languages was the message written?

Previous to Italian Guglielmo Marconi's time, telegraph signals were sent through wire. He invented wireless telegraphy in 1895. What is another name for wireless telegraphy?

Aaron Burr and Alexander Hamilton faced off in a duel with pistols in 1804 in Weehawken, New Jersey. Burr fatally wounded Hamilton. What high offices in government had these two men held?

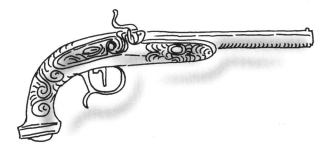

Louis Pasteur saved many lives when he discovered that germs spread diseases. By applying heat to milk, germs were killed and people did not get sick. What is this process called?

The Lewis and Clark expedition traveled through the Northwest to the Pacific Ocean and back. What river did they follow to its source?

Cyrus H. McCormick invented a horse-drawn reaping machine that could harvest 10 acres (4 hectares) of grain a day. What implements did people use to harvest grain before the reaping machine?

BALLOT

DISTRICT 1 DISTRICT 2

Elbridge Gerry was the only Vice-President whose name became part of the English language. As governor of the Commonwealth of Massachusetts, he signed a bill allowing voting districts to be divided to favor a specific party. What word describes this practice?

In 1891 a physical-education instructor, James Naismith, was asked by the head of his school's phys-ed department to create a sport that could be played indoors by several players during the winter. What was the sport he created?

Jean Laffite, a smuggler, pirate, and patriot from New Orleans, led a band of seafaring outlaws. After fighting for the United States with General Andrew Jackson at the Battle of New Orleans in 1815, he received a pardon. Which U.S. President pardoned him?

The Statue of Liberty is about fifteen stories high from its feet to the top of the torch. Who gave the Statue of Liberty to the people of the United States?

President James Monroe set forth the first major policy statement of the United States in 1823: the Monroe Doctrine. What was this policy?

Samuel Gompers left school when he was ten years old but by 1886, when he was thirty-six, he had organized a labor union of skilled craftsmen. He served as its president until 1924, with the exception of one year. What was the labor union?

The first college in the United States to accept both men and women was founded in 1833 and located in Ohio. What was the name of the school?

Alexander Graham Bell was the first to transmit human speech over a wire. He received a patent for the telephone when he was twenty-nine years old. For what did he prefer to be remembered?

The longest route for the westward expansion of the United States in the early 1800s was 2,000 miles (3,200 kilometers). What was the name of the route?

William H. Bonney, a cattle thief and killer known as "Billy the Kid," shot two deputies to death when he escaped from jail in 1881, just before his scheduled hanging. What was the name of the sheriff who tracked him down and killed him?

Presidents of the United States must be guarded from assassination. The first attempt on a President's life was by a mentally unbalanced house painter who fired pistols at a President at close range. They fortunately misfired. Who was the President the man tried to kill?

George Armstrong Custer, Civil War general and Indian fighter, had his last fight at the Battle of Little Bighorn on June 25, 1876.
Who defeated him?

History Challenge

A lawyer who gave up his practice in 1837 to devote his life to school reform became known as the Father of the Common Schools. What is his name?

LEVEL 2

77

History Challenge

Many U.S. citizens were disturbed because Secretary of State William H. Seward bought Alaska from Russia in 1867. They criticized him because they thought the land was only snow and ice. What did they call the purchase?

The Aroostook War of 1839, which was between lumbermen in New Brunswick, Canada, and the American state of Maine, is a war that never took place. What U.S. President settled the war without military force?

In what is now Manitoba, the settlers did not want the Red River Valley to come under Canadian government jurisdiction. This caused the Red River Rebellion of 1869 and 1870. The settlers were a mixture of white and Indian peoples. What were they called?

The first women's rights convention was held in Seneca Falls, New York. What did the women want?

In 1867 the Dominion of Canada was founded. Who was Canada's first Prime Minister?

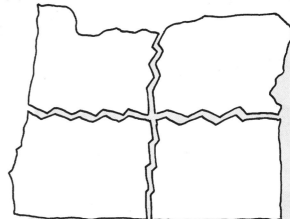

History Challenge

Four countries claimed some part of Oregon in the early 1800s. What were the four countries?

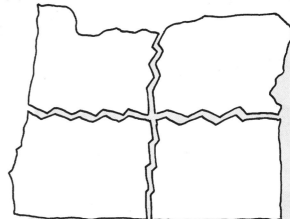

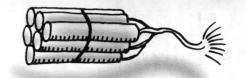

Dynamite is an explosive with many industrial uses. Invented in 1867 by a Swedish chemist, Alfred Nobel, dynamite made possible the construction of the Panama Canal, the carvings of the U.S. Presidents on Mount Rushmore, and the New York Subway system. What is the oily liquid that is the explosive in dynamite?

LEVEL 2

101

The first king to visit the United States was received by President Grant and given a reception by Congress. Who was he, and where was he from?

During 1857–1858 an American businessman, Cyrus W. Field, unsuccessfully tried to lay a transatlantic cable on the ocean floor connecting America with Europe by telegraph. In 1866 he was successful. What countries did he connect together with the line?

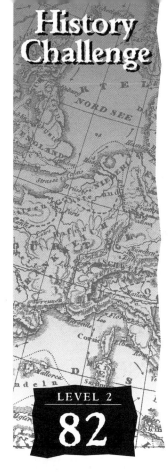

Florence Nightingale, a British nurse, became world-famous for her tireless efforts caring for wounded soldiers in the Crimean War. What award was she the first woman to receive?

Jesse James, train and bank robber during and after the Civil War, was the son of a Baptist minister. A reward of $5,000 was offered for the arrest of Jesse or his brother Frank. Who was the gang member who killed Jesse?

During the 1800s, boys and girls learned to read from textbooks written by American educator and clergyman William Holmes McGuffey. What was the name of these books?

Abraham Lincoln, sixteenth President of the United States, is considered by many to be the greatest of all the U.S. Presidents. In his Gettysburg address, what did Lincoln mean when he said, "that this nation, under God, shall have a new birth of freedom"?

Simón Bolívar, a famous South American general, won victories over Spain to win independence for Bolivia, Colombia, Ecuador, Peru, and Venezuela. What was he called by the South American people?

History Challenge

Appomattox Court House in Virginia was the site where the Civil War formally ended. Who were the two generals who signed the terms of the surrender?

LEVEL 2

97

The Texas Rangers were formally organized in 1835 as a group of mounted riflemen assigned to protect American settlers from Indians and Mexican bandits. What was the official uniform of the Texas Rangers?

The Emancipation Proclamation of January 1, 1863, ended slavery in the Confederate states fighting against the Union. What amendment to the Constitution ended slavery in every part of the United States?

In 1838–1839 the
United States government
forced the Cherokee Indians to move
from their homes in the Southeastern
states to Indian Territory in what is now
Oklahoma. Thousands died making the
trip. What was this forced march called?

Eleven slave states seceded from the Union to form their own government after Abraham Lincoln was elected President. What did they call their new government?

History Challenge

During the Mexican War of 1846–1848, United States Marines entered Mexico City and raised the American flag over the National Palace. The Marine Corps Hymn recounts this event in its first line. What are the words?

LEVEL 2

87

The oldest major religion on Earth is Judaism. There are about 13 million Jews. What was Judaism the first religion to teach?

Sir Richard Francis Burton, English soldier, explorer, and speaker of forty languages and dialects, was one of the few non-Muslims to gain entrance to Mecca and live to tell about it. What body of water did he discover in 1858 in Africa?

In 1859 John Brown, a radical abolitionist, attempted to free slaves by raiding the U.S. arsenal at Harpers Ferry, Virginia (now in West Virginia), to arm slaves who might rebel. Who captured him and his men?

A few years after the Mexican War, the United States bought a strip of land from Mexico for 10 million dollars. The land is now part of the southern ends of New Mexico and Arizona. What was the name of this agreement?

Dred Scott, a slave, lived for a while in areas where slavery was forbidden; therefore he sued to become a free man. The Supreme Court in 1857 denied him freedom. What happened to Scott when he was sold to a new owner?

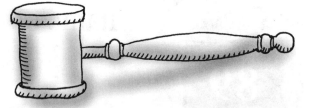

Isaac Merrit Singer designed a machine that sewed stitches continuously. Because the machine was expensive, he allowed people to make small regular payments after their first payment. What did this plan of purchasing become known as? What popular household machine did Singer invent?

In 1856 Margaretha Meyer Schurz began the first kindergarten in the United States. The teacher and children spoke German. In what town and state was the first kindergarten located?

1. The Bering Strait

2. America's pyramids had flat tops; Egypt's pyramids were pointed.

3. A human as a baby crawling on the ground, as a child, then as a person walking freely, and then as a person using a cane

4. Stonehenge

5. The central post office building in New York City

6. It is a tourist attraction.

7. Cuneiform

8. Moses

9. 25 miles (40 kilometers); He fell dead.

10. Grass

11. Nirvana

12. Aristotle

13. Papyrus

14. Cleopatra

15. *The Analects*

16. *The Hippocratic corpus* or *Hippocratic Collection*

17. Gladiators

18. Istanbul; Turkey

19. *The Justinian Code*

20. Muslims

21. Vinland (Wineland)

22. The Leaning Tower of Pisa

Answer Key

History Challenge

23. It became the framework for our Constitution.

24. Cliff dwellers

25. Children 10 to 18 years old

26. A vassal

27. Cathay

28. Genghis Khan

29. Lorenzo de' Medici

30. David

31. By fleas from infected rats

32. She was burned at the stake.

33. Land east of the 48° west longitude line

34. The Saint Lawrence River

35. Six times

36. *The Mona Lisa* and *The Last Supper*

37. Huguenots (French); Puritans (English)

38. Amerigo Vespucci

39. Martin Luther

40. The Strait of Magellan

41. Hernando de Soto

42. Leap year

43. England

44. *Romeo and Juliet*

45. Samuel de Champlain

46. Henry Hudson

47. Sieur des Groseilliers and Pierre Esprit Radisson

48. Tobacco

Answer Key

History Challenge

LEVEL 2

3

49. Thirteen

50. United Empire Loyalists

51. Taxation without representation

52. Responses will vary.

53. Rhode Island

54. Gravity

55. Harvard University

56. To adopt the modern way of life of people living west of Russia

57. Massachusetts

58. The Salem witchcraft trials

59. The First Amendment

60. Indigo

61. 1764; Responses will vary.

62. Cajuns

63. He paid off the last installment of the national debt.

64. Cockpit of the Revolution

65. The Bastille

66. Napoleon Bonaparte

67. The District of Columbia, now Washington, D.C.

68. The Rosetta Stone; Egyptian heiroglyphics, demotic (the popular language of Egypt at the time the stone was carved about 200 B.C.), and Greek.

69. Burr, Vice-President; Hamilton, Secretary of the Treasury

Answer Key

70. The Missouri River

71. Gerrymander

72. James Madison

73. European countries could no longer create new colonies in North and South America.

74. Oberlin College

75. The Oregon Trail

76. Andrew Jackson

77. Horace Mann

78. Martin Van Buren

79. Educational job opportunities and the right to vote

80. Russia, Spain, Great Britain, and the United States

81. David Kalakaua, King of the Sandwich Islands (Hawaii)

82. The British Order of Merit

83. The Eclectic Readers

84. *El Libertador* (The Liberator) and the "George Washington of South America"

85. There was none.

86. The Trail of Tears

87. "From the halls of Montezuma"

88. Lake Tanganyika

89. The Gadsden Purchase

90. The installment plan; the sewing machine

91. Watertown, Wisconsin

Answer Key

92. The new owner freed him.

93. Colonel Robert E. Lee

94. Belief in one God

95. The Confederate States of America

96. The Thirteenth Amendment

97. Ulysses S. Grant for the Union, and Robert E. Lee for the Confederacy

98. Responses will vary.

99. Robert Ford

100. Newfoundland and Ireland

101. Nitroglycerin

102. Sir John A. MacDonald

103. Métis

104. Seward's Folly

105. Sioux and Cheyenne warriors led by Crazy Horse and Sitting Bull

106. Pat Garrett

107. For his work as a teacher of the deaf

108. The American Federation of Labor (AFL)

109. The people of France

110. Basketball

111. Scythes and sickles

112. Pasteurization

113. Radio

114. Puerto Rico, Guam, and the Philippines

Answer Key

History Challenge

LEVEL 2

6

115. Motion pictures on celluloid film

116. The real McCoy, meaning "the real or genuine thing"

117. A one-dollar coin

118. Grover Cleveland

119. Fort Sill, Oklahoma; as a popular attraction at fairs

120. He developed hearing problems.

121. William McKinley

122. Her work in physics and chemistry

123. Girl Guides

124. Orville Wright

125. The National Association for the Advancement of Colored People (NAACP)

126. Vulcanization

127. Associate justice of the Supreme Court

128. Theodore Roosevelt

129. The Sixteenth Amendment

130. *The Birth of a Nation*

131. William Howard Taft

132. The United States of America

133. Warren Gamaliel Harding

134. United States of America, Confederate States of America, Republic of Texas, Mexico, France, and Spain

135. The Eighteenth Amendment

Answer Key

History Challenge

136. A dirigible, the *Norge*

137. *The Spirit of St. Louis*

138. The Nineteenth Amendment

139. Neurosis

140. Father of the Turks

141. Sending men to the moon on a Saturn 5 rocket

142. Corazón Aquino

143. Calvin Coolidge, Herbert Hoover, Franklin Roosevelt, and Harry Truman

144. Penicillin

145. The stock market crash on Wall Street in 1929

146. Sinclair Lewis

147. Bull market (rise); bear market (fall)

148. Wyoming; Franklin D. Roosevelt

149. Margaret Chase Smith

150. Georgia

151. Attu and Kiska

152. Midway Island

153. Volgograd

154. Prime Minister

155. Responses will vary.

156. Whether or not to drop the atomic bomb on Japan

157. Genocide

158. The atomic bomb

159. Democratic and communistic

160. Elvis Presley

161. Joseph McCarthy

Answer Key

162. He promoted peace through the European Recovery Program.

163. Gaul

164. The American Federation of Labor and the Congress of Industrial Organizations (AFL-CIO)

165. John F. Kennedy

166. *Sputnik*

167. Alaska, 49th; Hawaii, 50th

168. November 1989

169. Martin Luther King, Jr.

170. DDT (dichloro-diphenyl-trichloroethane)

171. The Vietnam War

172. Cape Town, South Africa

173. Responses will vary.

174. Fusion

175. Watergate

176. Nancy Landon Kassebaum; Kansas

177. President Ronald Reagan appointed Sandra Day O'Connor as an associate justice.

178. *Columbia*

179. Operation Desert Storm

180. President

Answer Key